Mule & Pear

Rachel Eliza Griffiths

New Issues Poetry & Prose

A Green Rose Book

New Issues Poetry & Prose
The College of Arts and Sciences
Western Michigan University
Kalamazoo, Michigan 49008

First Edition, 2011.

ISBN: 978-1-936970-01-8 (paperbound)

Library of Congress Cataloging-in-Publication Data:
Griffiths, Rachel Eliza
Mule & Pear/Rachel Eliza Griffiths
Library of Congress Control Number: 2011924070

Art Direction: Tricia Hennessy
Design: Kathleen Rissi
Production: Paul Sizer
                   The Design Center, Frostic School of Art
                   College of Fine Arts
                   Western Michigan University
Printing: McNaughton & Gunn, Inc.

Mule & Pear

Rachel Eliza Griffiths

New Issues

WESTERN MICHIGAN UNIVERSITY

Mule & Pear

Also by Rachel Eliza Griffiths

Miracle Arrhythmia
The Requited Distance

For My Mother and My Father

For Zora Neale Hurston, Toni Morrison,
& Every Outlaw Woman

For The Beautiful Ones
(often disguised as Books)
Who Have Lived Their Lives As Proof

Contents

Mule & Pear carries its title from Zora Neale Hurston's *Their Eyes Were Watching God*. I remain intrigued by an argument, between Janie and her Granny, regarding life, particularly womanhood. How each woman perceives the possibility and impossibility of a full life, given her conditions.

Many of these poems convey the intimacy I've developed and sustained through reading. From this act and all of its powers, my imagination gathered some of my most admired literary characters and their creators in one space, one intricate body, collapsing all restraints and divisions, in hopes that each voice would make its way towards other voices and I hoped, to me—a space that is ideal, flawed, intuitive, and intellectual. Thus making it, utterly, a very human space.

The poems clustered here are conversations, after-lives, interrogations, alternate endings, resurrections, bright detours, love-letters, rejections, desires, mid-wives, and what-ifs. Despite a seemingly broad historical and cultural arc, I found that the characters, mostly Black women, seemed to say as much to one another as they often have to me.

It is in the powers of such characters, however real and/or fictionalized, that I have understood much about literature. And living. It is in the music of their makers that I continue to re-read such stories for the language in which they were created and which, though some die in flesh and in spirit, will always live.

I ain't good-looking

And my hair ain't curls

But my mother, she give me something

It's going to carry me through this world

—Billie Holiday, "Billie's Blues"

I.

Mercy Does Not Mean Thank You

But say it is a body
with wounds

Say it is my father
bursting into tears alone
above his newspaper

Or it is the blood-flecked
underbelly of a rabid dog
named Thank You

Maybe it is the dark cinema
of my camera where I am

perched like a lamp
within the earth

Say it is four tongues
that puncture
a compass

& spin the points
of each season
towards a storm

Say it is new as a haircut
Say it is hard as a strawberry
Say it is useful as ugliness
Say it is necessary as hands

Say it is the vantage
from God's knees

Maybe it is the top ledge
of stone where one hundred madwomen leap
after eating their virginity

It is a moan beneath laughter
It is the gardenia pressing itself

like a white ear
to sad singing lips

And sometimes it is my mother
folded like a seed in the furrow
of the body's burning field

Perhaps it is the women
who smell like jasmine
& the liquor of melancholy

But say it is not like that at all

Then is it the white chickens
in milk crates clucking
near the butcher's window?

Or is it some scent that reeks
around the midnight hour?

Say it is the waterlogged
song of Emmett Till

Or is it an old man polishing
his skull with a blue handkerchief
on the subway?

And on my way to work
each day I pass a factory

of caskets noticing them
until I forget what they're for:

is that the pardon of memory?

But say this mercy is the ballad of girls
buried beneath a bombed-out church

Or a shadow removing
its eyeless hood

to become something else
that perceives goodness

Say it is the distinction of blood:

the unexpected
nose bleed

or axe of peace

lodged like an aneurysm in the brain
of a wild horse that must be put down

The song of a species
piercing earth's middle ear, drawing
blood & songs

But maybe it is not like that at all ·

Say it is a man's brown face
in the window of the White House

Say it is the speck of a cardinal
glimpsed through water

Say it is when our lips
finally touch after fighting

even though we are working
towards a type of kiss

that makes our teeth
click with ache

Say it is an elegy
for every hourglass

Or let it be a hand that breaks
the brands of suffering: a man's
shadow

that forces hooves
from his daughter's back

It might have been the jazz
Jonah heard in the whale's midnight
belly of three thousand fish

Or maybe it is a kind of depth
located in crow's ink

Say it is the crocus
grown up
near a poet's headstone

And listen to me now if you can:

If sometimes you must roll away
from my body's altar
taking my blood & poems

   enough

say to last you for the rest
of your life

I would not mind

I would not save
my knees from prayers

You cannot give my mercy back
: what you have taken
for yourself: needing it as much

as I have needed to give
it away

Sometimes you roll from me
as if you were afire

this one word

Against my body
you say Mercy: repeating:

    Have Mercy

because our bodies
are too merciful

because our bodies
are too small

Alice Paints the Moon

for Edward P. Jones, 2006

She lifted her dress
& it bowed. Shameful the womb
in the sky. Pale as the patrollers
who brought her back to the fields,
refusing to look where desire should have been.
Between her legs, maybe, is the madness.
A hemorrhaged world sliding down through her
skull & liver. She arrived, a dent in her head,
where a mule kicked her spirit into the middle
of some unknown world. Other slaves watched
as though they were gods. They tried
to wrap the sense of chains around her. She lifted
her dress. Behind the eclipse of sense
or madness she sketched against
the cave of self a Creation story.
She made life in their world look faded.
She drew it in colors it should have been.
Not black or white but blood. Wealth. The murmur of
those spirits flayed open like fevered horses.
In her dreams nobody is freed from the whip
unless they learn to speak from their saddles.
When the men catch her on the road they look up
to find the moon. Fearful when it is full & swollen
they can see her shape: a human shape. A free dancing
lunatic who still may be worth something.
Now with scarred feet she twirls jubilee. To the fields
boundless as the angels' fear: Master dead
Master dead Master *be* dead Master
died. White men, too poor to be masters,
still call the dead master Nigger Henry. Far easier
to ride away from evil when moonlight shone
through pine branches.

Sarah / Suckled by Her Mistress Manon Gaudet

When I gets to the North I gets more
than freedom. They gave me *cream*. Pure
work from a free beast
I didn't have to milk myself.

In the North they don't takes the rivers in my breasts,
the moon's wet nurse for my chillun. Sugar itself
is diff'rent too. Stolen angels flung from cane.

Everyone may have they privilege of sweetness
without the depraved eyes of relatives, masters
or mistresses, watching a slave's delight in a sip.

Let Manon think I'm a crazy, scheming,
uppity woman all she want. I got away, escaped
unlawful mouths sucking my secrets.

She catch a part of me again
but she can't catch all of me. Understand this:
I didn't offers my breast to her. The night she come
into my room like a man hunting my nipple.

No chillun of her own. No heirlooms
of opal milk for motherless lips.

Mistress knows nobody going listen
if I tell it. How can I tell
what's crazy or real anymore? White man.
White woman. White baby needs feeding.

Listen to me: *North folk asks if I'd takes sugar
and cream.* My shoulders never bowed. I speak
proper too: "Cream and sugar, thank you."

Black tea in a painted china cup.
"Please Madam, I'll takes three or four cubes."

(of their sweet white Jesus).

Esther Courts King Barlo

Wishes only make you restless. Emptiness
is a thing that grows by being moved.
—Jean Toomer, *Cane*

Any man bring fire like King Barlo
must have stolen it from him
or the Lord. Barlo gave me a tongue
of flame for my ears, deep down,
where virgins and their captors
sleep. Hear this: I'm burning
like a bush. I'm calling for you,
Barlo. Not my Daddy, not Moses.
My bush is burning. I'm a woman
of thorns waiting inside the husk
of my body. I'm born through your inferno.
Ask him, Jesus. Ask Barlo about the holocaust
of bodies. O God tell them where
we put our bones when work-fields yellow
like a wedding veil.

Jesus has been awhisperin strange words deep down,
O way down deep, deep in my ears.

A woman's glory?

It's far as stars: a dream of burden
men use when the world gets too big
and mule-eyes look back at them
from work.

Mirror, I see how color beats me.
Stole the gloss from Beauty.
Barlo will give it back to me.
I'm throwing fire in the river,
everything I've got. Let it come back
to Esther, if God pleases to remember
a pale girl who dreamt of fire.

Jesus has been awhisperin strange words deep down,
O way down deep, deep in my ears.

King Barlo, I tucked pearls and stones in my pocket.
Yellow skin doesn't mean my heart is less
blacker, Prophet. Flames take me like they taking
you. My blues is a halo. These years I've waited
for you, Barlo, is enough to make Satan wince.
You ever felt a halo round your finger?
You ever heard what burning grass cries
to the field that holds it captive?
I came into that old place, burning
strange for you, for you
to *save* me, Prophet.
All I got left is this hum:
don't think for two moments
I'm beyond begging.

King Barlo to Esther

This gal-oh-milk watch me from her window.
Say she needed me since she was nine.
But I know it was th sight of a prophet, on his knees,
face bathed in flames and saffron tobacco, that did it.
I knelt on th spittoon. Watched how th evening
word fell through th sky like a burnin god. I make flames,
roll anger from the sun. Show folks, white and indigo,
what be beyond clouds and comets of spit.
Gal-oh-milk couldn't never get dirty like that
if she tried her whole yellow life to find God.

This aint th place fer y. This aint th place fer y.

Gal-oh-milk, I aint th house fer y keepin.
Bottle-oh-milk cat. Y got to go back ter y fallutin Daddy.
Tell th man y milk aint sweet enough
for a real black king like me.
Y berries been dry since you was nine.
Crust-oh-bread and th eye of
a ham got more going on.

This aint th place fer y. This aint th place fer y.

Can't buy or change me like you do for th folk
your Daddy own. Since when my face look a church
storefront? Y couldn't make a fire with th kindlin
inside you. King Barlo aint th same as y Daddy
or y Jesus. That's how I know
when y came for me. You been worshippin
what you can't get at, can't understand.
That's 'zactly how I know:
y aint a woman yet.

Bought by the Bushel

The white master came
upon a field. In the center was a tree
and from it hung the ripe knowledge
tucked into the cores of apples
that had before belonged
to Before.

In the sky bluegrass rivers.
Mule-tailed currents cut the sun
into two worlds. In his bed
the master licked his lips
beneath sunlight.

Alice was there, free
and four-legged. A bull mounted
her and something made him watch.
Apple trees dropped fruits
into a field. The master stooped
to pick them up but realized
he also had four legs.

Nothing in his life frightened
him like the eyes of those
plowing beasts. Nothing held
its head against the yoke with that look
of vengeance. He stirred beneath
the coverlet of his quilt, erect
as his plantation rocked him
against a cat-shriek moon.

In the morning he watched his property.
Alice was abusing a mule that also belonged
to him. Nothing but hooves flashed
behind his blue eyes. Dirt words
crumbled from her lips. And this girl,
who the master remembered once
buying for cheap, held her caked hands
over her mouth as though mule
was her only language.

When a colored man came along
and offered him two hundred and twenty eight dollars
for her the master balked and brayed.
Alice could still work,
whether her sense was kicked loose
from its chain. He could not believe
the darkness of the skin
poised to buy a slave from him.

But when the two bushels of apples were set down
it was the color that made the deal seem better
than it really was. In the white man's dreams
the only difference was whether
the apples were green and not
the color of sweet autumns
or the bestial, bullwhip
wounds God inflicted
upon his back.

Dear Celie

One day I found you
lying facedown
in a bride-stain of indigo

the work field afire
with lilac torches

Some night
in a field of silk-
petal teeth
I found you
lying there
with sweet grass
humming
in your eyes

Shug's bee &
hive

Oaks knelt
beneath cross winds

Cotton blew white-
stringed breath
into dry miseries
where nets broke

& such plagued
frogs never leapt

One day Celie
the Lord's book
was like a fury of torn moths
flung to earth

through which the light
of womanhood
spilled through

& then these colored folk
words unhooked

an empty space
through which old mercy
shimmied
a lavender scent
gone dog bite

crazy

as Sofia was
when her neck
refused a heifer's leash
laughing at

the very idea —

you don't fit
a woman like Sofia
in no maid's
uniform

One day Celie
I want to find you
singing

I want to see
a smile knock
at each door
in your mouth

until somebody
answer us

I want to find you
speaking
your amethyst life

& shaking
your sparkle Celie

you can't fit a tree frog
into a woman hewn
from a flock
of battered humming
birds

don't let Mister
keep your hide company
with belts & backhanded
psalms

One day Celie
I found Him
wearing a robe
of plums

I found Him
singing
a blues
so deep
it was burgundy

I found Him
dreaming above
the work field

where you my sister
had lain

your life down
among the fallen
petals & razors

no more
cutting & sowing

a man's seed
that don't taste
like nothing

not even
the color of
your sister's
falling rain

not even of
our missing

our missing
the girls we was

girls beneath
wildflowers

The Native Widow's Proposal

1.

If I am no more than a girl, I manage buckets
of Ohio snow & laughter. A yoke of innocence balances
two shoulders. Evenings near wood fires
my mother pulls a bone-carved comb
through secrets tangled against her skull.

December snow is not absent.

2.

When the white men rode up on steaming
Horses I thought of no other syllable but *ghosts*.
Their eyes, aqua stones, sunk behind their sea-skin.
They inquired of land, ownership.

One of them observed my mother's head
as though anyone could claim that black swell.

Grandfather understood those eyes.
He told me to put animal skin into the fire.
          Push ash aside, he said. *Skin burns*.

He told me to pull up my hair
where it pressed the creases of my knees.
The children stopped laughing & eating
soda bread. They pointed at the horses' legs.
My mother gazed up at the sky: another winged place
she managed to defy.

Remember, grandfather said
without speaking. We offered them gifts, which they took.
We showed them the strong legs of our horses.

December snow is not absence.

3.

Day after day horse-backed shadows arrived.
On the seventh morning my mother would marry
General William Patrick Ian O'Shea. In the evening
she walked into the sky or ocean
while our grandmothers sewed her trousseau.

She left her hair in a heap outside
the door. No one found her. We would not try
to be displeased. Like a wolf she'd gone off
& died without peace. Freedom.

That night I made a hat with her abandoned fate.
Grief weaved the plumage of cardinals. Dove & quail.
Lost colors mourned my girlhood. Tomorrow
this General will take me to Cincinnati.

I will make hats & collect
white manners
until the absence melts.

4.

In the carriage my husband eyes me
with proper lust. I have bought my tribe
more time to plan rebellions. I think
of new hats & worlds, rolling away
                    from home, flames, blackened tendrils
of mother upon snow. I wear a fine lady's
coat of wool. Its buttons are not as bright
as grandfather's third eye.

          Remember, he repeated,
placing a pouch of secrets &
dead tendrils in my palm.

In the morning your ghost could be dead, Grandfather said
        without speaking.

Again I recall my husband's fingers
pulling, like shears, through my mother's hair.

I remember that day when my mother cleaved spirit
from flesh, that day when all the low bull-clouds howled
& shook ancestors down like poached tusks.

        The light will leave soon, snow filling its own

revenge. My heart,
under wool, flesh & buttons. Heart, I must be
occupied with absence

until newlywed passion
wears itself down.

I wear this hat because my hair is falling out, bald
scalp in December means freedom.

Celie's Notes: Dear God

in the white hook
of the swan &

in the eyelid
of Mister's dream

in the bucket
the straw broom

a family of washpins
that hang my life

to a broken line
of soap & water

in the husks

that wrap the heaviness
of corn so tightly

in Nettie's ghost
that spells vengeance
at Mister's shadow

in the sores that run
through my soul

in the mixing bowl
in the rising biscuits
in the pleasure of sleep

in Sofia's fist

in the legs of workhorses
a sea breeze before sunset &
the weary color of butter

in the slack breasts where
my babies' lips haunt me

in the snap peas
& the Christmas meat needing
to be dressed

in the onion's mercy
in the greens salted & boiled

'til they are soft & dark
as old glory-women

where sunlight rots the jail
and moonlight rots the bed

in this body where joy
waits tapping its bloodied toes

in this body where hard work
is a lean angel made of burlap

in the body where pain
drifts like feathers plucked
from a flying thing

in the way a stain of
purple insists on being
loved

in the way a soul
will not insist enough
on being loved

II.

Passing the Window

Some colorless breath blows mulatto snow past this window.
Opened or shut? Accident or not? There's a one-drop ghost
                        haunting the frame of this window.

What happened, they ask me again later. Did Clare Kendry fall?
Did she lean back into a white shawl of fallen gems?
I might have touched her. Can't say. Can't remember. Ask the window.

In a pale shroud of cool flakes the gold wick
smolders. Clare's laughter coiling its elegy through the sky:
constellation of an asp & siren. Fallen sting of height
                        from that window.

No more Nig. No further worry of the colorful secret.
Bellew would've done worse. Black curtains over windows.
Remember voiceless *Whites Only* signs in the window.

I might have pushed Sorry off the ledge too. Might have bared
my teeth as my fingertips tapped the flame near the window.
Why, I knew my place well enough. Why didn't she?

The tall French casements will keep this secret. The window
in my heart will need its glass replaced. Shattered and splattered
with blood, pride, race. *Continue to control my manners and my*
      husband.

On either side I exist. A suspect scale upon the sill of the window.
Too dark outside. Too light within. Or flip it
like a coin falling from a window.

Sula / Be Soft under Rock

Robins fell along rutted roads. Breasts
shuddering like pummeled fruits
from the plague of a woman's mouth.
All over the Bottoms language
bonded against its bondage.

When Sula returned, marked
with a hungry rose and red feathers
drifting from clotted clouds, a wild man
danced toward a collapsed mine of souls
where songs echoed like bats.

Shadrack won't you sing your *Always*.

When Sula pulled Ajax back from his skin,
the surprise itself killed her. Loam
gushed on the sheets where they writhed
in their own glares. His sugar funk
salted newer wounds. Old things,
without flames, burst into smoke.

She surrendered to a man
who never meant more than a taste
of soil. *Poison this thing inside you
that dreams venom.* Tomorrow
would cling to a boy she swung
beneath the river in a dream.

Splay the valves of this heart, Sula.
Soft as a mollusk. Cling, like emerald moss,
to the underbelly of stones
way beneath black rivers.

Stiff robins beyond
that boarded window
in the bedroom. Twilight singed
a bowl of oranges
in her grandmother's mind.
Softer tongues of
acid licking her. Love can kill
the flesh it craves.

Leg Done Gone / Eva Peace

My Hannah asking *Mamma did you ever love us*
as if her sense done gone.

I'll hear that question
for the rest of my days.

Yet I refuse to tell
the crippled mystery.

Perhaps I gave the limb up
for insurance, to the Lord
or the Devil: *does it matter now?*

I set Plum to fire
in his unmade bed
after he had gone
& returned from that war.

All the pretty boy
he was had gone.

Left life a burnt spoon,
glass of blood water
& blues records. Fire ignited

his dreams like an immolated eagle
while I fanned flames
with a ghost leg. Ghost love.

Soul flying somewhere
above Medallion, a song humming
without a mouth.

After BoyBoy left us
all the money was gone

& I inherited three beets
& my kids' hunger.

Middle of the night
when my will was gone

I crammed the only food
we had to eat
inside of Plum

to free the stone stools
that could have killed him
sooner.

Hannah,
flown now to the same fire
consumed my boy.

Love. Did I *love* you? Oh my.
                    You listening to me, girl?

I crawled on my knees with two whole legs
& asked for Mercy. My anger was gone

for two years. Had to leave my babies
with Mrs. Suggs while I learned to live

a cripple. *Freer than one might think.*

None of my beauty had gone
anywhere. Until I watched Hannah burn
out in the yard. Fire cursed

her skin: aroused like a blade
of loveless light. Sula stood
to the side of the house & watched.

Interested until the water was gone
& wasn't nothing but screams to save.
Bones to bury.

My life was flung
underwater. Same way Sula & that chile
swung Chicken Little to his death.

Flew to the river myself & heard
that snotty boy's laughter
as he flew from Sula's fingertips.

I went to his funeral
in a vision & dreamt
of Emmett Till.

After they put me
in that Sunnydale nursing home
I tried to get Nell to talk.

                    Tell the truth.

Surprise hissed through her
smile like a burn.

Gone & told her
straight: "*Me, I would've never watched.*"

The girl flew away, upset & left,
before I could give her some
of these oranges I keep
in my imagination.

My children ain't gone nowhere
from me really, you see. Plum & Hannah
& Sula & Pearl all
here in my universe.

They tell me things
about the past & future

when I think God's gone
in the present. Tell me
to come home to them.

*Come home
& love us*, they say.

Risa Takes a Look & Gives It Back

for August Wilson

Let them ask me
what I did: took a razor
to my legs.

Took a straight razor
to my legs

the way a man's tongue
will take a word
& cut you down

praise you
and the devil in the same
breath.

Let them ask me
about my legs again.

Here is a world
you don't know nothing
about: meanness in this earth
is as pleasurable as beauty.

Took a blue razor
to my legs & pulled

the blade

along like a cartographer
fixing a map against
the earth.

Here is a world
these fools of rust
can't change

no matter how loud
two trains might call
at midnight for a woman.

All day at work I play this song
until I feel Aretha
& I can dance

towards my own glory.

In the morning light
these scars is as new

& whole as a river waking beneath
the sun's lamp.

But don't get confused:

> *after midnight*
> *these scars know*
>
> *how to make a man*
> *weep for the moon.*

Pecola Breedlove Gives Geraldine
a Piece of Her Mind

for Elizabeth Alexander, 2006

1.

All the Geraldines of Ohio
gather in a parlor and serve me
macaroons, root beer with vanilla,
part my hair in eight sections
and lick my bald shame.

When the cat hit the wall I was sure it had enough
lives to keep its nature. What keeps you
hating the black you groom? I'm not sure.
Sometimes at night when the cats along the fence
shriek dirges and fuck the soft
bones that make their spines roll
like water do you get wet
along the lids of your eyes?

2.

This small black thing your son
wants to kill — that face of fur
slipping behind the radiator, is
the beast of your home. If I turned
your Bible over where you clawed
and stroked the leather, the white eyes of
doilies might attack me. Day after day,

I pushed hunger out the alley of my legs.

We all waited for the baby. It couldn't live. I prayed
for blue eyes. I'd be Shirley Temple dancing with Bo Jangles.
When my stomach got so swole it made plain
vision double, the women walked down sidewalks
with hands over their mouths, trapping
words away from their good dresses.

Could it live?

3.

I would like you to have this plate Do you like
my too-blue-to-sing eyes
Do you think my child will look like her father
my father a cracked plate secondhand
on a white windowsill near blueberry pie

A china plate edged with yellow trim
and sky-eyed cherubim—oh god

       (when Cholly doesn't—
             stop being
                  Daddy)

on the plate I washed iridescent suds and silence
while he crawled on his knees your Christian
women voices busy warming your own tombs

but on the plate a fleck of my skin dried brown
and blue fell soundlessly into old water
take these thoughts that mean nothing
to anybody without the color blue

Take this plate and feed the eyes
you can't stand to see
space of a black bitch you see
yourself Take this plate where my mind spoils
like meat Please don't let the cat be
anything but soft

Consolata Dreams of Risa

She entered the vice like a censored poet whose suspect
lexicon was too supple, too shocking to publish.
—Toni Morrison, *Paradise*

I'll take you to this city, Risa, & we can live electric.
Never crying again over our legs. Bring aloe.

Here, sterile smells of Mercurochrome & iodine
clean alleys where misery lingers. Judiciary rainbows.

Your name, *Risa*, floated up through a park I was carving
near my knees. A blade is far softer than a woman's mouth.

I live in their world but I exist here. Silent, serene enough
my wounds have no boundaries. Scabs mark
the territories of a woman's war.

Beg for neutrality, treaty & truce. I'll name a park & school
for you, Risa, when all the flooding has stopped. Not enough
tissue to catch this new country.

Foster boy from Mama Greer's home found this country
by accident when I was a baby girl. Trying to get himself into me
he dragged the jeans down my hips 'til the safety pin broke.

Etched a fine jag of roses along my stomach. Pink flower on my panties
made him lose his breath. His thing gets big. *Why*
do most people forgive the accidental wounds easier?

Now I make love in the dark. Keep the electricity off
so lovers don't see my kingdom. Name me a ruin.

Risa, you know how to do it too? Wield control like a mayor
with skeleton keys to a city of blood. Here's our blade
that keeps the peace.

What the Doll Says to Claudia MacTeer

This afternoon you broke
my head from the neck. Fingers
unloosed seams along my back,
ripping out the *Mama-mama* box.
I couldn't thank you enough.
Spittle frothed the edges of your lilac
lips. Attempt to destroy what isn't in me.
Brown fingers pressed into my wide blue
eyes. Sight no more or less innocent
than yours. Two feet stomped away
my nose. Pain in your toe did not stop
you from smiling. With bared teeth
you pulled the glue and black fringed eyelashes
away from my sockets. When the hard marble
eyes popped out, you scooped them up,
shoving jewels into your nappy pocket.
You ripped my curls out by the roots.
I didn't make any of this: the cotton
your great-great grandmother reaped,
tumbled out of me. You will be beaten.
They will not give you this gift again
unless you promise to love me as they do.
This ain't mine, is all you'll say.
Your mother called you in.
I stay out in the trees until another
finds me, puts me back together
so I'm me. At dinner your tongue
searches blue gums for the taste of
toy blood.

Dorcas to Violet: The Photograph on the Mantle Speaks

for Ai

Here you are trying to kill me again: a dead girl.
You & your raggedy husband taking
my slow dance away before the music
ended is what really hurt me in the end.

I was looking so goddamned good.

Death ain't my song. Resurrection is
for the living too. You ran into a typhoon
of blue snow with somebody's baby.
Parrots dripping from your widowed eyes,
your ears, that beak you call a mouth.
Jazz can pin you down like a man's pride. Shoot
your heart out into a night of white flaring
dresses. When your husband killed me
I had pulled the flats & sharps up my thighs
like garters. Listen how flesh snaps...

"Listen. I don't know who is that woman
singing but I know the words by heart."

Next time you remember you's just as country
as a rooster feather you ought to dance.
Don't you know how city life can cut you dead?
I'm grinding against hips of cement. Nothing ancient
there. You want to climb into my casket
& suck the straw beneath my face to taste
what you couldn't keep. Do the two-step before
my photograph, the one you placed before your husband
like a bowl of oranges. Arrange your own face
above the mantle & dance with that woman
whose name won't leave you. Talk to her
like you do them birds that bore you. Say *nothing* to cages.
Feathers & stones confess something bout burdens.
Tell how what weights us down in sleep don't matter.

"Listen. I don't know who is that woman singing but I know the words by heart."

Parting

Don't you let Joe Trace forget
the harm he done to himself
even if he can't feel nothing.

He ain't got a right to kill love
after it kill him.

Beauty got a price.
Don't you tell these women *that*?

Holding ears while these fools jump
from the blow of desire & grease.

What his sorrow got to do with me?
I ain't sad in death. I'm mad as hell.

Dixie Peach, Blue Magic, Red Devil
Lye. All those lies my hair won't ever keep.

What you give to sink your manicured fingers
into my scalp? Touch the kisses
your husband left there like suds.

I see you from where I'm at.

You want to get these chords. You there,
& crawling through your beauty

bags, stepping low then lifting careful
heels to fit my patent-leather shoes.

    Sometimes, Violet,
don't you hear another river
   beneath strains of jazz?

    What that blueness do
to your man? Shuddering
your fingers through my black hairs,

parting the hips that never let you
or your husband inside.

Violet in Snow

for Cyrus, 2006

I sit down because my face aches.
You know it's more than that.

All day I stand behind heads, coax grace
into finger waves. Shampoo trouble & misery.
Then I see a black baby in its carriage,

lonely as my breasts for the burden of milk.

That's not what I wanted: a mother's peace.
When my knife flashed behind that dead girl's ear,
all I wondered

was whether my husband heard me laughing.

Don't try to move my silence. I have a right to this
silken-cheeked baby, this street & doll mouth where love
& jazz meet, tip hats. Black gentlemen make bets

at who will win me. Skin my neck
with spit.

When they take the baby back
to that simple little girl I start to hum, slap
the face that fell down

from my skull. Beneath ribcage, a green parrot
repeats, *I love you.*

A beak peels my face from the street
because skin is helpless
& cannot fly away.

It's not as simple as that: feathers
& baby skin. A slip of

face. I am owed too little.

I sit down because the snow is heavy. Because
God's static makes no sound
until it falls through music. On the mantle

my husband & I worship her
young face. Beg our pardons.
There must be a way to make love to myself.

Other birds know the shrieks of escape. They fly
from coffins, bedrooms & cages. That little baby

needed me. Needed me to hold
life beneath the sway of snow.

Hagar's Last Witness

Today I passed a young woman on the street.
Wasn't nothing to be done for her.

Not my business
but I had to think about it.

Because after all
the girl was *pretty*.

Somebody's baby girl.
Make-up tracking railroads
across her face. Each wild feature

thrashing like a blackbird
near its last ecstasy.

Couldn't tell whether she was smiling
or crying. I slowed down. Stores was closing
and the lights were coming on
in houses for supper.

Wondered where she was coming from.
That kind of woman whose sorrows will follow
her body to a place where there's no trees for cover.

I didn't even want to pass her.
Exactly what a broken star might look like.

Think her name be Hagar
or something worse.

Wondered where her mother was
and why nobody had stopped that child
from staring into puddles of rain.

What was she going to see
in such muddy water –

a girl like that,
in a broken compact?

Brown paper buckling under
the rain's torrent where a bouquet of
colors trailed her hopes: sea-foam
edged nightgown and a white-with-a-band-
of-color Evan Picone number.

Girl like that can't see her face
even if prettiness itself twisted her arm.

No bothering with a mirror. No use in trying to
corral her into believing she could be
anything

but shattered. *Oh she was*
mimicking a mockingbird.

All that hair melting. Wet sugar
in the rain. Her eyes emptied out
in front of me like an hourglass.

Have you seen these time-struck
women on buses and trains, going
anywhere inside themselves but home?

Neat packages wrapped up in string.
Colored paper. Shade of lipstick
that make their words taste like fire.

Wasn't nothing to be done for her by now,
is the only thought I had as she passed me.

Got a whiff of the fever that she'd hold
in her arms the whole night through.

I would've held a woman like her in my arms
even if it meant we could both be
burnt up in perfume.

Saw a tube of lipstick near the curb
right before the bus run it over this morning.

Left a smear in its place
like something pretty
had been killed.

Hagar's Fever: A Lament

Look how I look. I look awful.
No wonder he didn't want me.
—Toni Morrison, *Song of Solomon*

What will be left for me after you take the sparrows
& your mouth? My empress breasts,
gourds of ash & milk, not enough.
These shoals of hair weigh my shoulders down,
coils of water filled with myrrh,
too nappy for you.

I smell like what I am: a woman. I gave you all
my pears. *No wonder. No*
wonder. You have chased life away in me
as winter hunts the leaves of fall.

What is a mountain without clouds?
You stuffed my fruit in your holy pockets, full
of nothing, trifling arrogant
nights. *If my thighs were the earth*
your life couldn't be enough.

How moonlight rivers the edges
of my lips, how fog tendrils valleys
early in the cold morning.

Guitar say I'm pretty. Reba say I'm hers. Pilate knows
what the earth is made of: bones & ugly
shimmering things.

Where did the woman go behind the mirror?

Guitar say I'm pretty black. Reba say I'm hers.
Pilate say *Hush baby* but I can't see where she went,
dancing across shattered glass lakes. The world
gave me sight instead of eyes. Take that mirror
away. Away across the lake.

The milk you left inside of me
is not sweet. What's growing now,
ain't safe. The mirrors— *Hush baby* —

lining up like gentleman, no
they are buzzards. Away across the lake.

Mama, give me lipstick. Give me shadows
for the lids of my eyes. Shadow blue & sweet as a drink
of arsenic. Give me silk panties for this old music
box. Give me garters, long & black
as syllable. Give me spider lashes & poppy
cheeks. I want to look like Cleopatra.
Give me cologne, vanilla talcum & red
lacquer for my toes. Give me the shine
of gloss for my lips. Give me scars
& lilies, I'm young, Mama. Don't
hush me. Don't hush

this. I need heels. I need patent leather heels
to cover my hooves. Give me lye
for my roots. Give me songs that don't make me
cry out for this man when I'm awake. Give me
a magnolia-pink ballad that will make him
weep my blood.

Mama, I don't love like a virgin. I don't laugh
like a tree of dancing larks. I don't say flight
& sea anymore when a man come
knocking for what he don't really want — *my music?*
I can fade like a braid of unwashed hair.

Look at those vultures, world.
Give me their knowledge.
How to wait death out. *How to rot
with grace.* Hush and listen.
They have Milkman's wings, his gift
for flight & deceit.

No, Mama, he don't want me.
He don't want me? Why don't he like
my hair? Why don't he love my tears?

No wonder he can't find me, vultures
high as mountains, all
around, all around
my fever.

Reba at the Funeral

for Miss Lucille

It ain't about your Christ having his way.
It ain't about pews glistening under

the gone-breath of my child. It ain't about black
people knowing more about true home-going.

It's about the gray-dove touching skin
that can't feel silk. Nothing's amazing

about grace or dying. *How young
is silence?*

It's about a mother, stitching closed
a child's eyelids. It's about throwing

out a broken tube of new red lipstick.
It's about what I had to give her,

which that flying nigger took, calmly
as a dollar bill in a gutter. Picked dreams
off my eyes.

How many houses grief need?
There's room in that casket for me. I said *loved*.
There's straw

under Hagar's cheeks. Somewhere
between her neck & shoulder blade

I could fit.

III.

Janie Talkin' in Her Sleep

for Zora

I swear on de life of a pear,
a part of me died
when mah finger,
like an enemy of de Lawd,
pulled de trigger
on mah sweet boy. How he
fell so hard. White rabid flowers
spinnin' their silence
to earth. Once he say to me,
"You must let de flowers
see yuh sometimes, heah
Janie?" But I keep on
wearin' blue, wearin'
blues 'cuz he lak me
lak de color's purity. I done gathered
de empty parts of de Lawd's ole gulf
an' strung an ancient net of gold-
flecked fish against my
skin to feed us tired souls.
Mah livin' days
full of holes an' starfish.
Mah son of Evening Sun,
mah teacake an' sweetbread,
mah star I buried lak a guitar
inside mah hips.

Guitar Soliloquy

The woman in blue overalls
rubbed her fingers over
my open mouth. A woman
whose eyes gone away
to a different time of blues.
Time before water. Time
before bite, dog & bullet.
She rubbed my neck,
murmuring, Us can't fly
Us can't fly, mah Teacake,
mah Sweetbread Boy. In my mouth
I tasted Lake Okechobee's apology,
forty miles wide & sixty miles long.
The jook of water washed
over my dusky jubilee.
This dead boy's old music box
lost somewhere in those waters.
I felt it all in her hands rubbing me
the night before she washed him
down for the last time, singing in his
ear. His ghost is here too, giving
me a try & hum. Both of them
weeping at this split of spirit.
Her hands gripped his stone-cold hands
around my throat, making angels
pluck their cat-gut lyres. Her hands
beckoned the brass ghosts of
Bahaman drummers to leap,
fly, walk along a field of low clouds
with dusty feet. *O morning woman,*
I want to say to her
when they get ready to pull the lid
over me & this boy. *O woman,*
I got to say, *love ain't even quiet in here.*
Not long as I'm in this boy's hands,
opening a strawberry mouth
over his half-smiling stitched lips.
Woman, me & this white silk
canopy, going to bear your man
'til he wake up again. When he wake up

again, singing to you. *Us can fly,*
heah Janie, Us can fly for certain.
Gal, just wait for us
to wake up in your arms.

Evangeline Beach

*People don't know how good
my daughter was. Pure her body was.*
—George Elliott Clarke, *George & Rue*

No turning from this erosion.
White bone, white wave, white
headstone. Rotting yields purity.
Drowning by the salt-wood
of mutilated figureheads
washed to shore.

In the throat of gulls, ivory
grief. The crying riffs of tide, grief
seething over limestone. Keep in time
with pain cake-walking the living blood.
Red silk fading into loam.
The loom of sky, the horizon,
all furious and taut.

The earth will have its elements.
Each hewn-breast is altered. The song
of altars arrives in salt and sunrise.
Let the laughter of dead and missing girls
herald dim sunsets. Bow, like courtesans,
to thunderstorms.

There will be more purging, altars
of flesh, without worshippers.
There will be another honeysuckle girl
who rides bareback, into a pink-limned
afterlife, anchored by her mothers.

Loquinn Jarvis Picks up the Knife

I seen the Jarvis gal go down when the bridge
went out. Her and her horse.
—George Elliott Clarke, *George & Rue*

We'll search f the body ——ice being
an elegant casket. Leave m her face.

That's mine too.

Easter came through
a woman's sea.

I never wanted
for her to ride that horse.

God of ice. God of low-
Accounts. No accountin.

Calla lily. Annunciated
angel. Horseback Madonna.

How do y kill a god? If we mirror
infidelity: Lord,

strike into ice. Shield her eyelids
from th frost.

Her body? Lost.

"You's to blame for this! Ya told Easter
to get that horse!"

Blamin god and a nigger is the same
mistake. Face of fool and trickster.

My spirit plunges into ice-beds. Hits
hooves. Water bein its bein.

My daughter's body?

Lost. Lost.

"Her body had been dissolving
in water. A lovely, delicate easy sculpture
of flesh and bone."

My sorrow clings like the sparrow
to its hymn. I cling.

No marriage for m baby.
No children either.

No road cobbled by memory. No
chile to bury me at the end.

You hear m anguish, girl?

She pull m hand in midair
when I took up
the butcher knife at Rue.

Blame holdin the hilt.

I could have saved more
lives if I had a killed Rue then.

If m rage wasn't feelin so cold
I would have turned the knife

into a rose and made his body
a garden.

Requiem / Easter

You will horseback night, always. In a canopy
                of ice. Marry slush with your betrothed
                        heart filling with greedy snow.
                              Know you were loved, as sunlight
is, by the prisoner on his last morning before
                                  hanging.

Your body pealing, the tongue of
                a bell, through the clabber of nature.
                          Thank the gods
of irony you'd never know what fully loved you: a man
                        whose hand was a hammer, an anvil, cacophony
on your half-piano.

                  Drowning, you come to surface.
Did you feel the horse slipping away in a waltz?
                  Did heartbeats keep a mean time inside flooded chambers?
Ice knew better. Beast knew better. Rue knew better
                      though he betted against the simple break
          of ice where you'd escaped.

You gambled on the impression of a surface,
                        a silver road that wound through dream,
guiding saddle, thighs and hoof.
                    You gave Rue a silver-buckled belt. Sweetmeats,
          yourself, full melody on a half piano.

Bessie: Drinking Desire

Never made me forget how hard life been.
Just made me smile 'til trouble's amber fingers soften my jaw.
And my dreams blur like a Southside midnight.

Brandy never made me coal inside the skull of a building.
Never made a man walk by without breaking his neck
to look back. Love never made my hips roll

        as though I could be sand,

sea, & tambourine all at once. Cold beer never made me say nothing
bad about how my mama tried to raise me. Never tried
to blame my daddy for running off with a yellow cattail woman.

Never made me think Bigger hadn't killed that white girl.
Trouble never made me forget I could always dance.

Liquor never made me feel like a decent woman. Never made me think
the world see me any less than they already did. A bitter drink never
made me think that Bigger wasn't going to kill me

one way or another whether I had already been living
dead any damn way. Drinks never left my palm lonely.

I never worried about sleeping in a bed of anonymity.
Never worried about Bigger doing right by me. Never

saw a drink walk off complaining about my nappy hair
or the stretch marks on my skin. Drinking never stole
anything I was already giving away or giving up.

Never seen a drink hate itself for being what it was.

                I was still alive in that shaft.

Never saw a shot of whiskey make a bullet
in my heart. Hangovers shape the soul toward forgiving.
Never going to forgive Bigger if I don't freeze to death first.

Never going to understand why trouble don't taste
good as champagne. Wonder why the midnight snow fell
slower than the tongue that froze
when he put his thing inside my *Don't*.

Bessie Explains the Evidence of Nobody-ness

I.

A long breathing of being nobody.
Forgotten 'til the cold season arrived.

> *I drank against owning emptiness. Anybody*
> *with knees can wash God's floor. But none*
> *with a mouth like mine can hold breath*
> this long.

> *Holding my lips together so words*
> *can't make hope. I drink until loneliness*
> *becomes another hiccup.*

The evidence you have right here:

An unspecific girl under this sheet.
Exposed. Black hands: the face of
a woman only a trace.

> *But I wasn't dead at the bottom of the shaft.*

Snowflakes hitting pale brains.
Court her with a brick.

Forget her bones will tell:

she didn't die.

Hatred left inside her like a ransom note.
The body a footnote to his crime:

> *bones in the furnace were loved more.*

In the glaze of smoke and snow a man digs through drifts
for his name and native tongue. His voice
crawled into her skull.

The proof of what he couldn't say?
What he tried to leave on the corner
for another nobody to pick up.

II.

I was your only woman.
        Woman, I said.

           (And the Trouble.)

                Bigger, don't do me like—

Innocent? Beneath the white sheet you can see
my mortis curves. White men called me
a peach even as they looked away.

              Head busted with a brick.

All you tasted was the pit of me,
the whiskey of me, the fear of
my content with shattered mirrors.

              I could see where I was going.

Through the craze of snow and the choir of rats
my body was not condemned. Like the building
where we hid and you stuck your nigger into me.

Remember the snow falling through the window?
The fear floating around until it melted
in our bellies? And the coldness in your body

and your voice as I cried No: no and now,
now after all you can't look at me: dead
in this courtroom of tipped scales?

Funnyhouse Haiku

For, like all educated Negroes—out of life and death essential—I find it necessary to maintain a stark fortress against recognition of myself.
—Adrienne Kennedy

Patrice Lumumba
piles of hair fall from my crown
a beast stares into mirrors

I want not to be
how dare the dead things return?
Black hair falls from crown

Creature of torment
Jesus in this jungle
Darkest one near light

White mother Black face
Frankopenny trees bleed now
Forgive my father

Queen Victoria tells me
A stallion raped us
I must bear this race

They killed Lumumba
Blaze of Christian kerosene
Brightest of them all

Darkest of them all
My bald heart nears mirrors
Who's hair belongs where?

Kiss of the Queen Bee

"Mama, where does the bee sting?"
"Your heart," Mama says.
"Down in your draws," says Miss Billie.
Is your heart in your draws?
—Gayle Jones, *Eva's Man*

Felt like milkweed Dead
eel Anvil   Popsicle stick Anchor
of flesh   Devil's forked tail
White stuff pearling
from its cocked grin
milkweed & sweet plum
streaming juice
between my teeth   Meat of apple
Cabbage Blood orange
New cologne of period &
mustard seeping through
my teeth

Isn't this what Davis wanted
all this time: holding me up
in that room? Feeding me
until the only thing I craved
was flesh? Waiting captive
& unclean for this?

What kind of
woman are you
what kind of
decent woman
would do . . .

Wasn't bleeding
enough

Fixing me a plate,
he said "when vinegar touch
the egg it smells like . . .
a woman's smell."

Now I'm sitting   *tearing the boy plum*
in their prison cell   *my mouth sings an elegy*
but I'm free   *peace of mind*
the queen bee's labor   *between my legs*
put to some use   *what kind of*
I ask for a comb   *woman are you*
My hair won't stop   *no kind of woman*
snaking from its roots   *like you should love*
Inconsolable   *a man*
Lion & Medusa

But it's only the males
who grow the full crown
of gold moss
show who's boss man
who fucks
the pride

                                 I sat next to the queen bee as a girl.
                                 This is how your hive works,
                                         she kept whispering
                                         'til my ears swell like lilies.

Davis said
"Egg's
the same thing
a woman's got
up inside her."
"That's why
it smells
that way.
It smells
like fuck."

Way she buzzed the heart
with a blade. She stung,
left a stain
of honey & blood
behind
her heart
after she ripped
*it ou*t

Sitting in this cell
Elvira's laughter
slips the bars
between my legs
Elvira knows
how to remove
our scabs   *Wasn't bleeding*
Some women know   *enough*
how to fill their own
graves
No suspect   *My cramps*
No newspaper   *wrenched the heart*
can relay this   *until it bled*
news: why
I bit   *So hard*
                             they get so hard

                    Lost Miss Billie's bracelet
            when I was eight. Heard Daddy tear
              Mama's clothes off. Calm enough,

                    he smiled at me before
                    he closed their bedroom door
                    to teach us both a lesson:

desire & whores don't have
nothing to do
with the other.

The detectives
don't trouble with me
except to ask
the same question
A hard-on fear
keeps their brass buttons
official
Looking at me
they touch their guns

I keep asking for a comb

Freddy Smoot gave me
a pearl-handled knife
& kissed my cheek
He'd played a game
twisting a popsicle stick
up inside of me

Ghost of milkweed
tickles my throat
Police see me
worse than a dead man
Nothing's hated more
than a larceny-hearted
woman How could any woman
kill a man like that?

When I lost Miss Billie's
bracelet
I couldn't protect
the shadow
of a girl whose life resembled
a long sting.

Never found
the answer
to this before the queen bee
stung herself to death

the man she really loved
left her alone
spoiling
in her own
honey

"I wanted
to ask how
they could make love to her
if they knew
they were going to die."

IV.

The Problem of Describing Mercy

for Aisha & Aracelis

Consider the taste
of muscadines clinging
to a stem. That taste of color

a globe of water
opening your mouth's
power.

Teeth tear it, cursing
the tongue's work.

But mercy is not like that.

Beneath piano lids. Fingernails.
Some kind of filth.

How it might fit like a raspberry seed
along the wall of your molar.

Could you see it then? Without a telescope
from the windows of a moving train?

Why must the mule starve
to death in a field of sunflowers?

The mouth of a thing
that licks your wounds,
its teeth bared (just in case).

Consider the vows of hands
or the work of knuckles.

But mercy is not like that.

Epigraphs of sand pass through
at the waist. Breaking
the horizon of wire.

In a field of sunflowers
I saw a mule lie down.

And from its stall of bones
a shadow rose & covered
the length of the beast's cries.
But mercy is not like that.

I pressed my face against the window
of this train, fear running

a woman's mind upon the looping sutures
of grief. The apparition of light
settles dark animals into peace.

I fly apart inside an hourglass.

Blues for Sweet Thing

> *Who's little girl am I?*
> *Anyone who has money to buy.*
> *What do they call me?*
> —Nina Simone, "Four Women"

I'm honeysuckle.
A girl child crying
holy seven sins.

A harp & loom.
A rack of ribs.
A ribcage.

A pocket of coins
never to be spent
because my country

no longer exists. Almanac,
without page numbers

or prophecy.
For you I was sycamore,

pear, willow,
maple & bougainvillea.

For you
I was bathwater.

Gazelle, artichoke,
tulip & daffodil.

Your father's tears.

Blue fern of smoke
from a cigarette

opened by a fist
of summer rain.

For you
I was a red dress.

Teeth that glowed
under the hot bulb
of a basement party.

I was a sacrificial smile burning off
lamb's fat after midnight.

Ace & diamond.

The good time
no clock could find.

White sheet. A pearl drop earring.
Shadow wearing her mother's hat.

Birdcage. A bird who sat inside
your ears like a wound

until clarity sounded
its back-break trumpet.

A woman gone to church
with no stockings.

A woman gone to love
wearing no lingerie.

No skin either.

Your memories pulled apart
by a boll weevil's testimony.

For you
I was all these things.

I ended up
being

honeysuckle threading
a ghetto fence.

Dandelion crushed
between a cement wall.

The rapper's accessory.
A bank's vault.

I know more
about the sadness in paper

than the hands that
crush paper into clouds.

                              Ghost
of magnolia.

How did I end up
being a ghost of every
nothing?

I was a sweet thing
until the moon was sobbing

along the stairwell tower
of some woman's throat.

Elegy: Breath: Eyes:

Memory be closer to me
now that you are leaving

      You captive admirer —
      You terrorist —
      You circus acrobat —
           twirling in a hundred costumes

One day you'll be buried
Blackbirds will sing

while leaves fall
over the other closed vault

I can't remember this now — *what*
was it like not to forget
who I was?

Be beyond me as a song is
         beyond me

       You are inescapable
as the sun

Merciless as the moon
when you refuse to dream

       You courtesan —

Your face beneath water
         moving away

Breathing life
into you

makes it hard
to imagine you living
without me

For My Future Headstone

for Adrienne Rich

I translate the vagaries of
                      stone: my heart
has no limbs

elsewhere   In another country

a woman's life is marked
by the absence of rocks

Only later will the rains inscribe
      memory:
                  life in cuneiforms

I don't know which
      birds will dart their blurs

over the words   Over
    her last body   A vow
          of stone

Ordinary light is her last privilege

A parrot rustles its green *caw*
    in the city where I am not waking: more

of the old anonymity

    I held her hands & feet: death
    worked its frost evenly within

a bowl of water
as I washed her knees

& throat   A humming

passed over her body's flower:
My ears search for pitch

Do I dream of silence?

Requiem

Do not name your grief
for this burning village
of lights where the eyes of
girls are ruined by darkness.
The lanterns of foreigners have
burned the roofs of girlhood
into brass and straw idols.
These daughters who wear
your aches. Old exiles
whose dreams live
in smoke. The wildfire of
terrorism spreads a mirage.
This mouth searches the rubble of
memory where the unborn scream
for guns. Do not ask what
the soldiers did. Do not ask
the mirrors for the after
birth. There was a child
who escaped her mother.
Soldiers, armed as midwives
with sheets and orders, searched
beneath coverlets of smoke
for breasts. Calabashes of milk
tinged with ash. Sugar. Name your grief
for the memory of ancestors.
See if you can wash their blood
from your government
uniforms.

La Tête du Soleil

for Chimamanda Ngozi Adichie

Baby, baby in your mama's calabash.
Reed grave of ghosts, Moses & grain.

With your thick hair parted and plaited
for its journey through the exiled trains, black
rivers spooling their thread within

the wounded. Childhood lingering
under the sun's belly.

Baby of kola & palm wine, baby
whose eyes will never close
to Mama's Igbo lullabies.

Girlhood buried in some anonymous grave
where the rest of you disappeared
like a drop of blood.

Baby, baby in your basket of war.
                    Ndo. Ndo, baby.

In a basket your laughter
once piled. Cassava and yam.

Down the river. Jesus Christ
saw the head of his cousin placed
on a sterling platter of everlasting Amens.

A child's head rolling inside the gutted basket.

Inside memory the daughter's head rolls
her name through gray lips.

Hair in perfect blurry pleats.
Ndo. Ndo. Ndo.

Words do not have the weight
of a thousand silent heads.

Bayonets carved the sun's victory.
The roads, the roads of war.

A small ebony head
your mother shows to anyone.

Her hands slippery on the red stem
of your baby neck

as she dragged an old saw
across your collarbone.

I beg your pardon. I beg
your pardon. Lord,
I beg your pardon.

A mother's eyes greet a yellow sun
& curse its head of tarnished gold.

Her claw upon the lid
of the basket as she lifts it
to sing to her own child's head.

Never to bury this
song & sun.

Never.

Self Portrait / This Dust Road

        is behind
& beyond
      at once

a sort of luminous
intersection: crucified

upon the body

My spine is an orchid
& through my flesh

      a clean line pushes

through the full mouth
& wild mind

This road tended
by element

      & cracked at its fault

I go on
daughter & salt

Unlined now & slow-snaked
        as sunlight traces grooves
          at the base of dust

I'm walking with seven hundred hawks
above my head

And in the warm pit
      there tremors a song
    of deep things

leaving their prints
upon my heart

Memory will be
behind & beyond the ash lamps

But let me go on in this dark

Memory will be
        another thing yesterday

& tomorrow

I will be a memory turning
        down my lamp to watch
the snowfall at night

In this distance
        there are cities & villages alike

where light wanders like a feather

        or body seeking shelter

The skies inside of me are crowded
            with owls: the interrogation

of these selves after mid-life

        Or between the leaps

of youth as it ran away

        to ride another horse

There will be
no more questions or bridles

            & in some cities
there will be no more birds

        Where will I land next?

As often as the sun drops
below its apology

This odyssey
    makes it way
through crab orchards
       & alleys of hanging dresses

My blue bedroom fills
      with the promise
         of shells
My spine an orchid

      My hands firm as loaves
      My lips bright & wild

         as jacarandas' full meaning

      Orchard where the thoughts wait
        to fall & be

         eaten by the deer

But let me go on:

    there is a surging of
         so many inconsolable hooves
     near the bluffs

The cliff of my heart
    is jagged ballast blue

subtle as a sky
      in its loneliness

     I sit within the arms
        of a great dust

Don't ask me
about the road anymore

     I've walked & crawled
upon a red-brown path

Orchids filling my ears
　　　　with bent music
　　　　　　　I go until the going is my journey

Leaning towards the body disfigured by memory
I read the score of fossils & mollusks

　　　　　　the useless horns & broken teeth

　　　　　　　　　Praise the sight
of unbroken eggs: rain drops

　　　　beading black wire: clasped

hands on street corners: lost
balloons strangled in tree branches:

　　　　　the certainty of the path
　　　　　beneath memory

There are enough translations
of the tongue's frailty

　　I go on
& my sisters & brothers of tongue
　　　　speak this map

when I'm upon my knees
　　　& desperate to eat my own secrets

　　　　I go on

& my mothers & fathers of tongue
　　　wield their knives & hammers

Their shadows lengthen
　　　　upon the earth

I am enough

    for a thimble

               Breaking apart

    until I touch the bottom

of my soul: the shell
        of a word

      rolling away
        like a dream

This body

      is a kind of volume
      demanding another space

Praise the fields of mules
whose spines adorned
with spring petals

See the train & a woman's face
      floating in a square of light

I pass a frayed rope
        hanging from a tree
where a great weight

        has given way

A ghost scar stretches
      along the peninsula of my hips
where the birth still connects me

          to that other place

to the Before
      & against the After

I crouch at the lip

                  of dust

The world in a knot

                  at the root

Notes:

"Alice Paints the Moon Mad": "I met a dead man layin in Massa lane/ Ask that dead man what his name/He raised he bony head and took off his hat/He told me this, he told me that." Edward P. Jones, *The Known World*

"Sarah / Suckled by Her Mistress Manon Gaudet": "When you gets to the North," she said, "they invites you to the dining room, and they asks you to sit at the table. Then they offers you a cup of tea, and they asks, 'Do you want cream and sugar?'" Valerie Martin, *Property*.

The following lines are taken from Jean Toomer's *Cane*: "Jesus has been awhisperin strange words deep down, O way down deep, deep in my ears" and "This aint th place fer y." The poem is dedicated to Nikky Finney.

"Dear Celie" and "Celie's Notes: Dear God," are dedicated to Alice Walker.

"The Native Widow's Proposal" is dedicated to Rita Dove and Patricia Smith (2006).

"Passing the Window": "Death by misadventure, I'm inclined to believe. Let's go up and have another look at that window." Nella Larsen, *Passing*.

"Dorcas to Violet: The Photograph on the Mantle Speaks": "Listen. I don't know who is that woman singing but I know the words by heart." Toni Morrison, *Jazz*.

"Reba at the Funeral": "Somebody's been botherin my sweet sugar lumpkin. Somebody's been botherin my sweet baby girl." Toni Morrison, *Song of Solomon*.

"Janie Talkin' in Her Sleep" takes the following: "You must let de flowers see yuh sometimes, heah Janie?" from Zora Neale Hurston's *Their Eyes Were Watching God*.

"Guitar Soliloquy" takes the following phrase: "Us can't fly" from Zora Neale Hurston's *Their Eyes Were Watching God*.

"Loquinn Jarvis Picks up the Knife" takes the following phrases: "You's to blame for this! Ya told Easter to get that horse!" and "Her body had been dissolving in water. A lovely, delicate easy sculpture of flesh and bone" from George Elliott Clarke's, *George & Rue*.

The poem, "Funnyhouse Haiku" is a found poem, incorporating lines from Adrienne Kennedy's play, *Funnyhouse of a Negro*. The poem is dedicated to her.

In the poem "Kiss of the Queen Bee" the lines which appear in quotation marks are direct quotations from Gayle Jones' novel, *Eva's Man*. The poem is dedicated to her.

"The Problem of Describing Mercy" is an echo of Robert Hass' poem titled "The Problem of Describing Color".

"Blues for Sweet Thing" refers to the figure of "Sweet Thing" in Nina Simone's song "Four Women."

The title of the poem "Elegy: Breath: Eyes:" is a direct echo of the title of Edwidge Danticat's novel: *Breath, Eyes, Memory*. The poem is dedicated to her.

"La Tête du Soleil": ". . . and she describes the child's head inside: scruffy braids falling across the dark brown face, eyes completely white, eerily open, a mouth, in a small surprised O." Chimamanda Ngozi Adichie, *Half of a Yellow Sun*

"La Tête du Soleil": "Lord, I beg your pardon," is from Toni Morrison's *Beloved*.

"This Road": This poem is dedicated to numerous mothers, sisters, men, and women whose names I didn't know but who helped and hoped me *be*.

Acknowledgments:

Earlier versions of these poems appeared in the following journals:

African American Review: "Hagar's Fever: A Lament," "Alice Paints the Moon Mad," "La Tête du Soleil," "Janie Talkin' in Her Sleep," "Guitar Soliloquy," and "Celie's Notes: Dear God"

Aunt Chloe: "What the Doll Says to Claudia MacTeer," "Dear Celie," and "Consolata Dreams of Risa"

The Drunken Boat: "Passing the Window," "Elegy: Breath: Eyes:," and "Funnyhouse Haiku"

PMS: poem memoir story: "Pecola Breedlove Gives Geraldine a Piece of Her Mind," and "Requiem"

Proud Flesh: "Sula, Be Soft under Rock," "Bessie: Drinking Desire," "Reba at the Funeral," "Esther Courts King Barlo," and "Parting"

Second Run: "Hagar's Fever: A Lament"

Immeasurable gratitude goes directly to my family, my friends and poets (both), and my mentors. To the tribes of poets, living and dead, who continue to teach me. I also thank the institutions and organizations that have given me their full support during the completion of this work. Finally, I could not have imagined, conjured, or dreamt any of these poems without the original creators of these books, these extraordinary stories and women that I have read literally and figuratively, and utterly respect with all of my heart. Thank you.

Rachel Eliza Griffiths is the author of *Miracle Arrhythmia* (Willow Books) and *The Requited Distance* (Sheep Meadow Press). She received her M.F.A. in Creative Writing from Sarah Lawrence College and her M.A. in English Literature from the University of Delaware. Her work has appeared in *Callaloo, Crab Orchard Review, Indiana Review, RATTLE, Brilliant Corners, Puerto Del Sol,* and many other journals. A Cave Canem Fellow, she is the recipient of fellowships from Provincetown Fine Arts Work Center, Vermont Studio Center, New York State Summer Writers Institute, the Cave Canem Foundation and others. A photographer and painter, her visual work has been published widely in both national and international magazines and journals. She teaches at Sarah Lawrence College and lives in New York.